A

Jill

FROM

Christie, Elliot
Mike + Miraida
With love +
thanks ⊗

OTHER GIFTBOOKS BY HELEN EXLEY

In Times of Trouble
Thank You to a very special Mother
Thank You to a very special Dad

Thank You to a very special Friend
Thank You for Every Little Thing
Words on Kindness

Published simultaneously in 2001 by Exley Publications Ltd in Great Britain and Exley
Publications LLC in the USA.

12 11 10 9 8 7 6 5 4 3 2 1

Illustrations © Lincoln Exley Designs 2001
Selection and arrangement copyright © Helen Exley 2001
The moral right of the author has been asserted

ISBN 1-86187-125-2

Edited and words selected by Helen Exley
Illustrated by Sarah Jones
Printed in China

Exley Publications Ltd, 16 Chalk Hill, Watford, Herts, WD19 4BG, UK.
Exley Publications LLC, 232 Madison Avenue, Suite 1409, NY 10016, USA.

ACKNOWLEDGEMENTS: The publishers are grateful for permission to reproduce copyright
material. Whilst every reasonable effort has been made to trace copyright holders, the publishers
would be pleased to hear from any not here acknowledged. *Pam Brown, Samantha David, Jenny
de Vries, Pamela Dugdale, Marion Garretty, Stuart & Linda Macfarlane, Ingeborg Nelson, Maya
V Patel, Pushpa Patel, Helen Thomson, Margot Thomson* published with permission © 2001.
Helen Exley © 2001.

THE
THANK YOU
BOOK

A HELEN EXLEY GIFTBOOK

NEW YORK • WATFORD, UK

What "thank you" means

"Thank you" are two of the most
wonderful words a person
can say or hear.
Every time someone says,
"Thank You" the world becomes
a little more beautiful.

STUART AND LINDA MACFARLANE

"Thank you" recognizes kindness in another person. That kindness can be a small thoughtful gift, or it could be a huge sacrifice like saving a life or giving constant love and care. It's one of the nicest phrases in any language because it recognizes that warm touch, the art of human generosity large or small that makes our lives worth living.

HELEN EXLEY

SPOILT ROTTEN!

When I open the presents
WHOOPEE!
That makes me smile.

PUSHIPA KARAI, AGE 10

Too much of a good thing
is wonderful.

LIBERACE (1919-1987)

Somehow you know

that giving should be

more fun than receiving

but it isn't.

CHARLOTTE BEATTIE

AGE 10

"THANK YOU"

*Two little words offered in return
for an extraordinary range of objects and acts.
"Thank you" to an aunt for a pair
of ill-fitting socks. "Thank you" to a driver
who stops to let you cross the road.
"Thankyou" to a neighbour who has found
your lost child.*

FIONA AND PAUL HANDLEY

Super pressies!

For all the little,
sudden,
unexpected surprises –
thank you.

PAM BROWN, b.1928

How can you say, "It was nothing!?"
It was everything to me.
It meant the world. Thank you.

SAMANTHA DAVID

Kindnesses

are like summer flowers

slipped between the pages

of a book – their messages

of affection springing to life

again in a few years.

PAM BROWN, b.1928

LITTLE THINGS

Here's to all the little things,
the "done-and-then-forgotten"
things,Those
"oh-it's-simply-nothing" things
That make life worth the fight.

AUTHOR UNKNOWN

Even the smallest act of kindness
says "I care",
says "You matter", says
"I thought of you".
And so lifts the heart.

JENNY DE VRIES

No act of kindness,
no matter how small,
is ever wasted.

AESOP

For all your unconditional love,
joy, enthusiasm, and for all
you've given me this year,
as my friend and my stalwart
support - thank you.

PAM GILLON

ALWAYS ON MY SIDE

There are a sprinkling of people
who give flowers when you've just
come second, who quietly smooth
over your worst muddles, who help
when you don't necessarily expect
or deserve kindness.
Thank you!

HELEN THOMSON, b.1943

You make all the right noises

when I phone you

with some tale of woe.

It's good to know that someone

is always on my side.

PAMELA DUGDALE

For simply being you

Thank you
for simply being you –
constant in friendship,
unfailing in kindness.

JANE SWAN, b.1943

"*Thank You*"

I could shout the words from the highest
mountain for all the world to hear.
I could paint the words across the moon
for all the world to see.
I could cast the words in bronze
for all the world to feel.
But, however I proclaim my thanks,
there is no way to fully show
how grateful I am.

STUART MACFARLANE

... FOR BELIEVING IN ME

Confidence. Excellence. Fun. Strength. Generosity. These are the great gifts you gave to me. Thank you!

MARION GARRETTY

You believe in me.
There are no trite words of
thanks that could tell you
what that means to me.

INGEBORG NELSON

I am so very ordinary.
Thank you for making
me feel special.

PAM BROWN, b.1928

A 'THANK YOU' FOR THOUGHTFULNESS

I'm not grateful so much for the gift, nor even for the sending of it.

I'm grateful for your thought, your selflessness. I appreciate those above all else.

EMILY MORTON

SMILES AND KINDNESS

Life is not made up of great sacrifices and duties, but of little things; in which smiles and kindness given habitually are what win and preserve the heart.

SIR HUMPHRY DAVY

(1778-1829)

A look of sympathy,

of encouragement;

a hand reached out

in kindness.

all else is secondary.

MAYA V. PATEL, b.1928

THANK YOU FOR BEING
A REAL FRIEND

To fall down you manage alone
but it takes friendly hands
to get up.

YIDDISH PROVERB

A real friend is one who walks in
when the rest of the world walks out.

WALTER WINCHELL

ONLY YOU REMEMBERED!

We all could have dropped in for a chat,
washed a few dishes, fed the cat.
Run errands. Matched the knitting skein.
Climbed those long stairs up to the lonely flat.
We all meant to.
(Tomorrow is such an easy word to say.)
You did these things for me when
I was in trouble... eased fear and pain.
Thank you for that.

PAM BROWN, b.1928

THAT ILLOGICAL ACT OF KINDNESS

The world should say thank you

to that amazing band of people

who always give that uncalled for,

illogical acts of kindness.

HELEN THOMSON, b.1943

When a person does a good deed
when he or she didn't have to,
God looks down and smiles
and says,
"For this moment alone,
it was worth creating
the world."

THE TALMUD

YOU!

You gave yourself.

That was more important than all

the kindness and time you gave.

These would have been empty

without that gift of part of you.

MARGOT THOMSON

YOU GIVE ME LOTS OF MONEY AND LOTS
OF PRESENTS TOO, BUT I'D RATHER GO WITHOUT
THEM AND HAVE YOU.

SHIRLEY GARDEN, AGE 10

How far that little candle throws his beams! So shines a good deed in a naughty world.

WILLIAM SHAKESPEARE
(1564-1616)

*A THANK YOU
FOR GIVING
JUST AT THE RIGHT
MOMENT*

I thought I was alone;

then someone sent me flowers.

CHRISTINA ANELLO

*Generosity lies less in giving much
than in giving at the right moment.*

JEAN DE LA BRUYÈRE

... FOR STANDING BY ME

*I can never thank you enough because you
have been there,
you have stood beside me,
you have propped me up,
and let me down gently.
You have rebuilt me and made me strong.
I am a tower of your thoughts
and care. Thank you.*

GREETINGS CARD INSCRIPTION

KIND HUGS, GENTLE TOUCHES,

ENDLESS DAYS OF SUPPORT —

THEY HAVE FORTIFIED MY LIFE.

AND NO WORDS CAN EXPRESS HOW

MUCH THEY MEANT TO ME.

THANK YOU.

HELEN EXLEY

... BEING THOUGHTFUL

Thank you for knowing
what needs doing, and doing it.
Whether it's giving a hug,
or a bandage, or a cup
of tea. Or just knowing when
to do nothing.

SARAH NELSON

THE KIND PERSON UNDERSTANDS A NEED
BEFORE IT'S SPOKEN — AND ANSWERS IT
SO QUIETLY IT SEEMS COINCIDENCE.

PAM BROWN, b.1928

With a close friend one need
never stretch one's eyes and
say "Just what I wanted",
For it always is what you wanted.

CHARLOTTE GRAY

FOR ALL THE LIVES
YOU BRIGHTEN...

This greeting is not just from me –
but from the garden birds you feed and
the cats you stroke and the dogs you talk to;
from the small, wild four-footed things you
help through the very cold winters.
From the trees you prune and the seedlings
that you nurture.
From the people who are cheered by your smile.
From all the lives you touch and brighten.

PAM BROWN, b.1928

THANK YOU FOR YOUR COMFORT

For your deep kindness, great thanks.

HELEN FITZWALTER-READ

I suppose I could have struggled
through without you.
But thank heavens I didn't have to.

PAM BROWN, b.1928

No one is as capable of gratitude
as one who has emerged from
the kingdom of night.

ELIE WIESEL, b.1928

*Littlest kindnesses repeated
a thousand times
have the greatest value.*

PUSHPA PATEL

*For the twenty-two
thousand or so smiles.
For the years of hugs,
forgivings and kind words,
thank you.*

MARGOT THOMSON

When I am sick you are so kind
to me, you tuck me up
in the rocking chair with my
crocheted blanket and then get
me a nice, hot drink.
When I am not sick you are
just as kind to me.

HELEN HUGHES,
AGE 10,
TO HER GRANDMOTHER

No need to speak

The kindness I have longest remembered

has been of this sort, the sort unsaid;

so far behind the speaker's lips that

almost it already lay in my heart.

It did not have far to go to be communicated.

HENRY DAVID THOREAU
(1817-1862)

THANK YOU FOR BEING THERE FOR ME

It is not so much our friends' help that helps us as the confident knowledge that they will help us.

EPICURUS
(341-270 BC)

THANK YOU FOR BEING WITH US THROUGH IT ALL — FOR THE WARM PRESSURE OF YOUR LOVE AND THE IMMEDIACY OF YOUR GRACE.

DOUGLAS GIFFORD

You were always there.
No one else was.

HELEN EXLEY

... THANKING YOU FOR YOUR TIME

*Thank you
for taking time
to listen to me
when I want to
tell you something.*

SHIRLEY GARDEN,
AGE 10

TO THE KIND PEOPLE
WHO MAKE OUR WORLD

Thank you to all the people

in the world who are always

ten percent kinder

than they need to be.

That's what really makes

the world go round.

HELEN EXLEY

This is what sets this tiny

opal of a planet off from

a million greater worlds –

the possibility of kindness –

the possibility of care.

PAM BROWN, b.1928